TRACI DEMOSS BYERLY

UNAPOLOGETICALLY GRAY

UNAPOLOGETICALLY GRAY

Traci DeMoss Byerly

Photographer: Rebekah Maynard | www.rebekahmaynard.com

Makeup By: Jenine Galante | Instagram - @j9gala

Pearly Gates Publishing LLC

INSPIRING CHRISTIAN AUTHORS TO BE AUTHORS

Pearly Gates Publishing, LLC, Houston, Texas

Traci DeMoss Byerly

Unapologetically Gray

ISBN13: 978-1-947445-40-6
Library of Congress Control Number: 2018962112

Scripture reference is taken from the King James Version of the Holy Bible
and used with permission from Zondervan via Biblegateway.com.
Public Domain

Disclaimer:
The purpose of this book is strictly to inspire, entertain, and inform readers.
It is not intended to diagnose or be a substitute for emotional or mental health
care. The author nor publisher are in no way responsible for or liable to anyone
because of misuse or outcomes resulting directly or indirectly from
the decisions made by readers regarding this book.

For information and bulk ordering, contact:
Pearly Gates Publishing, LLC
Angela Edwards, CEO
P.O. Box 62287
Houston, TX 77205
BestSeller@PearlyGatesPublishing.com

Dedication

Unapologetically Gray

is dedicated to all my sisters and brothers
who constantly hear,

"Why don't you just dye your hair?

You are too {fill in the blank} for that gray!

It makes you look so {fill in the blank}!

You would {fill in the blank}

if you didn't have all that gray hair!"

Acknowledgments

First and foremost, I want to thank my personal Lord and Savior, **Jesus Christ**, for having patience with me as I finally fulfilled His gift to me to write!

I also bless God for my gift that He gave me: My own Boaz named **Fredrick Byerly**! You honor who I am designed to be and my calling. You did not stand in the way. You MADE the way, so I could do whatever I needed to get this project done. I thank you for your encouragement, accountability, and prodding to keep me moving when my motivation dipped. I appreciate your support and covering more than you'll ever know.

To my nucleus world that started with my parents and siblings: You all were my first audience and cheerleaders in life. I am so thankful for all of you!

To my parents, **Chester and Linda DeMoss**: Thank you for always encouraging me to flow in my love for writing.

To my siblings, **Ingrid and Chester, II**: Thank you all for your patience and support for all the times I pressured you to listen to whatever came out of my head.

To my daughter, **Giordaun**: You are my reason to be the best that I can be. I do this for you, baby girl! Thank you for your patience for all of the time it took for your Momma to grow up and into her destiny. I am here to cheer you on as you continue to write your testimony and grow to flow in your giftings.

To my bonus children, **Adaire, Cameron, and Hailey**, and bonus grandson, **Carter**: Thank you for unconditionally accepting my family into your world. I love the connection that I have with each of you. I treasure you all in my heart as my own children. Most of all, thank you for allowing me to be **UNAPOLOGETICALLY** me!

To my Texas bestie, **Michele Hayes**: You have been on me to write a book for at least a decade. I know you thought I wasn't listening! Thank you for your patience and encouragement during the times I tried to make my rut as my grave, as well as my fight to get out and come back stronger than ever. I am so thankful to have you on this crazy journey with me.

To my cousin, **Tonya Smith**: Thank you for spending hours on the phone with me to help me properly construct this book. You truly have a gift of bringing order to things!

To my precious aunt in Heaven, **Bishop Dr. Aletha Cushinberry**: You were also one of my greatest cheerleaders who believed in me and my writings. I know you are smiling down on me, and I have made you proud. I hear you saying, "Guh, it's about time!" I miss you dearly!

There are so many family and friends whom I have not mentioned by name, but you know who you are. I love and thank you all for being a part of my transformation from unbecoming to becoming who God has called me to be and do.

Prologue

Hi Love,

There is a story behind your distinctive existence. You **ARE** chosen to be a wonder. If you do not already know why, you owe it to yourself to learn what makes you so special because you truly are. You are powerful in your own right, even if you don't feel it, see it or know it yet. You were designed to silence the foolish talk about whatever makes people uncomfortable with you—without lifting a finger. You, in your extraordinarily-fashioned way, have a divine purpose to **BE** exactly as you are.

I hope this book inspires you to find your voice, liberty, protection, and love for yourself to clearly express your uniqueness and focus on your whole best being. You do not have to be obnoxious to prove your boldness—unless that is just your innate personality. Most people believe they must be confrontational to make their presence known, but that is not necessary for you. We have all heard that saying, "Meekness is great strength under control."

You **ARE** good enough. You have nothing to prove. No more shrinking back or hiding. Do not let the voice of ignorance shut you up and have the final say about you. Speak up to amplify the best of you! Live your best life, and be **UNAPOLOGETICALLY** you!

Signed,

~ *Unapologetically Gray* ~

Introduction

What is it about you that makes society so uncomfortable? Is it how you were born? Is it a natural transition due to maturity or growth? What about something you were born with or without? Is it something about your physique? A gap between your teeth? Your skin color or no color at all? Body parts and facial features that are uniquely shaped? Skin discolorations? The texture of your hair? Gray hair?

Regardless of what others think or even what we think, these unique characteristics, parts, and marks were given to us. It was somehow predestined that we are unique. We can handle whatever it is, no matter what. We did not ask to be the peculiar ones in the bunch. We did not plan, plant, paint, or remove anything to get these distinguishing characteristics about us. Still, this is us in and with our uniqueness. It is all good — whether anybody likes it or not.

Why are **WE** apologizing, feeling disgraced, and trying to conform to a society that does not care about the people on whom they impose their unreasonable "cookie-cutter" standards? Deeper than that, why should we carry the burdens of others being uncomfortable with us or parts of us?

Whether we realize it or not, we practice a form of daily abandonment when we cover up or deny parts of us that are considered "undesirable" to others. Just know that we are not doing this to our bodies only: We are also neglecting and abusing our inner selves (spirits, souls, or whatever your preference) who know our true beauty, handsomeness, worth, potential, and strengths.

Did I just strike a nerve that is buried deep in hurt? Rejection? Denial? Resentment? Shame? An "I-don't-give-a-care" attitude, yet you are still secretly succumbing to society's rules with guilt? No, I will not call out specific scenarios. If what I said made you uncomfortable or offended, please keep reading.

You know who you are. Know this, my beloved: You were chosen to take what society deems as shameful, unworthy, and unlovely and use "it" to blow to smithereens everything they think is right in their own eyes. This book is purposely and lovingly made for you and all your uniqueness, as well as for those of you who cast your views upon others without careful thought given to your impact. I sure wished I would have had this book several years ago.

While writing this book, I got an epiphany about something I had never identified before until now. My revelation was that I was a 6th-grade girl stuck inside an adult's body. Classmates unmercifully and repeatedly teased me about my appearance. My hair and body size were the reasons why! I was a very skinny, shapeless little girl with very short hair that was cut off due to a bad box perm. That unloveliness seed planted within me by classmates had grown up with me into full-blown feelings of insecurity and inadequacy as a 43-year-old woman! My appearance was once again being criticized, but by friends and acquaintances. During my introspective

UNAPOLOGETICALLY Gray

moment in the mirror, I observed those in my past who took great pleasure in seeing how far I would go to be accepted. The root of the problem was not them. It was because I did not know or like myself.

That was the turning point of what I called my "rebellion against the world." It sure lit a fire in me! I refused to jump through any more hoops about my appearance that were not conducive to me or my life. I have done the little 6th-grader justice and brought healing to her. She's now a feisty woman who loves her total being!

I am so thankful for my initiated self-proclamation of rebellion against the dictates of beauty standards that often disregards gray hair and other nonconforming looks. My "Aha!" moment manifested at this thought: Even if I entertained trying to keep up with dying my hair and could no longer afford it, then what? I came to grips with my gray being a part of me, but I refused to let it be the negative focus of me. Self-care became extremely important because I knew I had to be healthy in order to prove a point. Although my inner work intended to prove something to others, I later learned that it was predominantly for my personal growth and healing. I will share more about all of that throughout this book.

My work consisted of gaining the emotional fortitude to withstand foolishness. I developed a well-defined mentality to be confident in who I am with my looks. It also included the discipline of physical and spiritual maintenance to defy the naysayers by growing the resolve to protect myself and not buckle at verbal attacks. What started as a self-esteem issue developed into self-love, and love found me!

[xii]

At the time of my transformation, I was a single woman who wanted to be desired. I hardly felt I could ever be accepted for me. Always hearing suggestions to alter myself in order to fit someone else's needs got really tiresome. Too often, within the first meeting or when someone got comfortable with me, I heard, "You are so beautiful, but that gray hair! It just…" I heard it about my fluctuating weight as well. I wanted someone to focus on more than just my looks—like my heart and mind….**ME!**

Now, I am a greatly-blessed woman with a husband who would not have my hair color any other way. Although my packaging and wrapping paper was very pleasing to him, that was not all that caught his attention. My gray hair, along with my inner spirit and wisdom, were among the top things that made me attractive to him! My prayer was answered for someone to see more than just my outer appearance. He loves my total being as much as I do! I do not believe this could have happened if I was in hiding or loathing myself for who I was designed to be at that moment. I loved me enough, and that confidence made me lovely.

Understand this: True self-love—not narcissism—makes a person beautiful to others because love begets love. More than anything, I am blown away at the thought that my gray hair journey would inspire me to write an **UNAPOLOGETIC** manual for those whom society says, "Your appearance doesn't make the cut!"

I know the divine appointment for the release of this book is right now. People, especially those in authority who do not practice proper use of their power, exercise their freedom of speech privileges to say whatever they want and however they want. I want to be the voice of those who feel beaten or pressured to change something about their natural appearances all because other people are uncomfortable or have strong preferences.

Watch me get this party started! Hear me **ROAR** as I take my liberties with my voice to express my divine right to exist in my gray glory! It begins right here. Right now!

TABLE OF CONTENTS

Chapter One

UNAPOLOGETICALLY GRAY

Gray hair—whether anybody likes it or not—is like a child who has been conceived. That seed is planted within and will surely make its debut. Like birthing and keeping a child, gray hair is a choice.

Did I just boldly compare birthing a child into this world to gray hair? Is it really that serious? Yes, it sure is.

Children and gray hair will come to most people. They are a natural part of life. Both will come at an appointed time, often unknown to us. For some, they come very early, and for others, they come much later. Some choose to delay the process and then make it happen on their own terms. People have choices whether to keep, conceal, or get rid of babies and gray hair. People also have hardcore opinions about either choice.

You are probably forming an opinion right now as you read the last few statements thus far.

Depending on whose presence I am in, the following analogy may appear harsh. Nonetheless, I am made to feel that way about my choice to have gray hair. It seems like our society places as much (if not more) emphasis on appearances (looks, performances, and possessions) than on babies and the elderly being allowed to live life with value and positive, unconditional regard. It should not have to be this way.

Did I strike some emotions? Take a deep breath and breathe. I am going somewhere with this.

The point of the matter with the comparison is that we all have our deep-seated convictions and personal choices about our children and gray hair. Just as people are comfortable with parenthood, many are very comfortable in their skin with their gray hair. Our decision to be gray is often a hot topic that takes place among family, friends, and strangers; in the corporate world; in salons; among society and in the media; and alone in front of mirrors. We are often so caught off guard with the off-colored questions about our hair and suggestions to alter it that we are either left speechless or respond defensively. No one has the right to force their beliefs, judgments, standards, and personifications on anyone. We cannot wear others' lack of comfortability about our hair. We should not be forced to conform to a society that does not care about our histories, our make-ups, our health, our self-esteems, and our desires. There are countless reasons we proudly embrace our gray glory.

Welcome to **MY** private world of "graydom" and why I choose to go against the standards of society while being true to myself!

Gray is a universal sign of celebrating our existence. Many religions and cultures embrace aging. Gray hair is referenced in the Bible's Book of Proverbs as being the glory of old age, beautiful, and a sign of wisdom. It is evidence that we are still here and standing strong, despite rough pasts. Even if we did not have it hard, we are living good lives and grace is upon us.

For many like me, premature graying genetics have been passed down to us. It tickles me when I get senior citizen discounts based on assumptions that I am one. I still get blessed whenever I correct them about my age because they thought I might be offended at the offer. Maybe gray-haired people should be carded, too?

We have a responsibility to show a society that fights so vehemently against aging that we can mature gracefully and powerfully. Contrary to popular belief, we do not have to look or feel old, run down, and haggardly. As a matter of fact, the majority of us are not that way. Perceptions about aging are based on either negative or positive beliefs, as well as who we watched grow older. This is my charge to those of you who are struggling with showing your signs of aging. It is beneficial to research what a lifestyle of healthiness and vitality looks like by the people who are organically living it. It can be natural **and** attractive!

You are in the midst of a journey. Let no one discourage you with their alleged labels of wear-and-tear. You stop it, too! Gray hair is a sign of fortitude and experience. Focus on the great image you were created in to live out. Be that image with excellence and celebrate you! You obviously have time. Change your lenses to reflect the gorgeous person you are with your sign of spiritual splendor, no matter what your culture or religious beliefs are. Your internal light further adds illumination to your gray that is matchless (no pun intended).

Women's hair is often referred to as our "glory." My sisters, please let this saturate your minds, your inner selves, and your self-esteems. Think about it: What is usually among the first things noticed on us that attracts a lot of attention? A beautiful hairstyle? Sure! A beautiful crown of gray hair? Absolutely! Gray hair is a natural tiara. A queen never walks with her head held down in shame. Adjustments such as a flattering hairstyle will help with custom fitting a tiara, but there is no need to be self-conscious about a silver or white head. Every tiara is different. Like fingerprints, they are created specifically for the individual queen donning it. It is much different than the pretty lace-fronts, exotic add-ons, and eye-catching hair dyes that are absolutely gorgeous. One downside I see is that they produce cookie-cutter products. It all looks very similar, no matter who is wearing them or which style the hair is worn. Not to mention, these products also have potentially damaging effects with prolonged or improper use.

Be free and bold with the graydom! Express what is the real **YOU**! Queen, you have established your reign. It is time to become comfortable with your natural royalty! You can pull this off by growing your confidence in having a positive attitude about your whole person and your life. Although the queen's tiara is eye-catching, she knows there is more to her than that. Her tiara does not define her, but it is one of her most important accessories that is meant to be worn proudly. Show your gray and yourself majestically!

Furthermore, just like diamonds or other precious stones, pieces of wood, or pottery that has been carefully selected for exhibition, gray hair is the same way. It is a natural creation to be displayed. It is not manufactured by man, so no one can take credit for it. Nobody really has the right to judge what people's imperfections and flaws are — unless they are God (or your belief of a higher being or power). The last I checked, my God made me in His image and knew my end from my beginning. I am **GOOD** with my premature gray!

What is considered as flawed often adds more character and makes it "one-of-a-kind." It is beautiful in the eyes of the beholders. The primary beholders of this beauty should be us! If we aren't sold on it first, no one else will be, either. Society wants to remove all flaws to the point of people and things becoming or looking artificial. We choose to accept what has long been rejected — our gray hair — as well as other original parts and marks. We are human beings, not Barbie dolls that can be molded, manipulated, and replicated to look like everyone else. Barbie indirectly brings up a very strong point that we all could take heed to. Follow me on this for a moment...

The media and a vast majority of mainstream beauty industries are the utmost abusive to us, yet we submit to them whether we intend to or not. Even if we dismiss or frown upon this brutal truth, it remains. Low self-esteem is the crack that invites the abuse in which was probably created many moons ago. We carry internal poisonous landmines until we are either set free or take it to our graves. Anytime someone has something negative to say to us, we self-destruct with an implosion or explosion. Come on! Don't act like you have never heard of people who live most of their lives like this! A wrong trip (no pun intended) on those landmines cause us to say and do destructive things to ourselves and those around us, but I digress.

The media and certain industries take on the persona of a gang of mean girls as they prey on weaknesses. They dichotomize our body types, skin tones, features, and hair. We are subliminally bullied into conformity to look like the prototype of the season, or we are purposely excluded out of their plans. If we do conform, it does not matter if we look like a hot mess, as long as we spend the money to make them rich. Consequently, if we do not comply or look the part, we are blown off as social outcasts.

Our society assumes two positions:

1. Turn a blind eye and deaf ear to the abuse; or
2. Side with the media and industries to further snub those who do not follow or look "the type."

This is not to be taken lightly or as an exaggeration. The "wrong look" of people in their natural states can cost them jobs or promotions, places to live, financial backing, relationships, respect, decent representations in the media, and more. With the masses thoughtlessly backing those who discriminate, it is hard for victimized parties to feel validated and fully supported. Catch my drift?

My heart goes out to those who are forced to look like something they are not. They believe they cannot show or be the true expression of themselves because of how they look. This fuels self-hatred, which is not fair. It's time for a change.

We refuse to be objectified to fit other people's standards. Our focus is not just on the packaging or the wrapping paper of our appearances with the gray decorations on top, but the real gifts inside. We often face so much discrimination that people miss out on some real treasures — the essence of who we are. Does it feel good? Nope! But we are resilient. You will find with many of us that we are true to ourselves, and we own our sense of freedom. Most people who cannot be seen publicly in their perceived undesirable natural state do not possess this type of freedom. We all know people who go into hiding or become downright angry if they are forced to be exposed in their natural states.

For those of you challenging that last statement, please do not take offense as I ask the following questions:

➤ Can you look yourself squarely in the mirror and fully accept your perceived flaws?

> ➢ Are you willing to candidly evaluate and decipher what are valid reasons or excuses for what you dislike about you?
> ➢ Are you prepared to renounce all of your invalid excuses to cover up and choose not to conceal your perceived flaws ever again?
> ➢ Above all, can you truly appreciate yourself in the nakedness of those flaws?
> ➢ How much unconditional love do you have for your total being? No, really. It is not just for the external appearances that you maintain so well.

I am not judging you at all. I have had major struggles with my own appearance. There is so much love and compassion in my heart for you, and no condemnation whatsoever. Prayerfully, you answered those questions honestly. It is okay if you might have some work to do. Please know that you are not alone.

Now, I do understand there are legitimate reasons for certain decisions made to keep perceived flaws under wraps. On the other hand, it will be a whole new paradigm shift, especially when you have a strong drive from other forces to look like someone or something you are not to fit some mode of perceived normalcy or to be accepted by people. It will be tough not to draw attention to yourselves as you choose to uncover and fully embrace living authentically free in your skin. Trust me, I know. I have the t-shirts and souvenirs for this process. It is perfectly fine to acknowledge this and deal with it in your own time. However, may I caution those of you who delay the process and continue to deny parts or all of yourselves? You probably have a sphere of influence who look up to you or may want to imitate you. Those who genuinely care about you depend on you to be true to yourself in whatever way that may be. More often than not, your life is not about you anyway. You are to be an example for someone or something else. Whether you choose to do you or something else, that reality still lingers with you.

There are also times when people's lives teach us exactly what **NOT** to do. If you still prefer to cover up and build walls, please be real about your motives. At least be able to receive the stripped version of who you are and what you look like in your private time. Speak the truth and loving words about you. This is the key to some inner healing.

We **ALL** have things about us that do not sit well with some majority somewhere. I know I have categories that I could fit in to be **UNAPOLOGETIC** for. I will use my gray hair journey to demonstrate my personal **UNAPOLOGETIC** movement.

Let me preface my personal story by saying this: I am not knocking people who want to wear weaves, wigs, extensions, dyes, falsies, get injections or surgeries to enhance parts or features, and so on. As I stated earlier, there are times when these decisions might be necessary. Also, let me reiterate that for many of you, I recognize your need to have a better quality of life. It is one thing if you dislike a perceived flaw and it does not cause self-loathing. It is something entirely different if you dislike yourself because of other people's preferences. I am specifically addressing those who either need to be free from abusive internal and external beliefs or have no idea that they are projecting their uncomfortable views on others. Who knows? I may even be an inspiration to those of you who are on the fence to be free about whatever society has influenced you not to like about yourself.

Regardless, I am a staunch believer of people exercising their choices. Please do not infringe upon my choices. We should be able to appreciate diversity, which is often the problem with our society and their need for conversion and conformity of the people. Let's transition to an **UNAPOLOGETIC** state, shall we?

Chapter Two

THE UNAPOLOGETIC WORLD

My hope is that this book serves as your mirror. You have a safe space to snatch off the covers. It is here that you either recognize or remember that you are a person and not parts. Please feel free to write in it, use it as your study guide, and read it often. You deserve inner healing and self-love beyond the surface of your appearance and, most of all, to embrace your total being. I am here to remind you of what you already know and stir you to action. As you read this book, see where you can identify yourself and answer the following questions:

> ➤ What can I do to make sure my wellness needs are met so that I flourish and live **UNAPOLOGETICALLY** in my skin?
> ➤ In what ways can I establish my worth and boundaries, yet still maintain an atmosphere of dignity?

> ➢ How can I build a bridge that draws people out of stereotypical, biased thinking towards the advancement of a more harmonious environment?
> ➢ Am I willing to create a supportive community (tribe, family, etc.) that provides support and strength for one another within, as well as promote inspiration and unity on the outside?

Throughout this book, you will see **UNAPOLOGETIC** or **UNAPOLOGETICALLY** in capitalized bold font when it is referenced in its right framework. Sometimes, we need the volume turned up in print to get the message. It takes boldness to stand up and make yourself, as well as your voice, your purpose, and your life shine. I am simply here to put fire to your pilot light.

My encouragement is for you to live an **UNAPOLOGETIC** lifestyle from the inside out. No, I do not have all the answers. I can ask questions to inspire ideas within you, which may point you in the right direction. You just take that baton of ideas and run forward to confidently create a magnificent movement or community within your sphere of influence. There are certain principles to living this lifestyle, which I am more than happy to explain. It is easier to tell you first what is *NOT* creating the **UNAPOLOGETIC** culture that I am conveying. None of the following are truly my heart or the basis for this book if you choose to be unapologetically:

> ➢ Evil, hateful, and violent.
> ➢ Exclusive with the intent to harm and neglect others.

- ➢ "Unnecessary" or "extra" with attention-getting antics that draw negativity.
- ➢ Someone or something that you were not meant to be or do.
- ➢ Less than mediocre in attitudes to justify who you are or what you do, instead of getting help to deal with your pain or immaturity.
- ➢ Anything that goes against treating yourself **AND** anyone else with dignity and respect.

I personally cannot take credit for or endorse those activities, which are either the sources or outcomes that go against the grain of the **UNAPOLOGETIC** culture. In your opportunity to be unapologetic, would you consider doing you in a manner that is healthy and loving to yourself with a refusal to add any more dysfunction to this society? Do not put the book down yet because you will miss something! Familial and societal issues substantially increase because hurting people hurt people.

I am cognizant about the large majority of people who have absolutely no issues with being careless. They are unapologetically downright destructive with their words and choices of actions. These are often the very same people who have something inconsiderate to say about others. It definitely makes matters worse when wounded people draw negative attention as they retaliate against those who hurt them. I totally get it, but revenge is not always the primary remedy of living an **UNAPOLOGETIC** life in the face of ignorance. Think about this on all sides. The root of this cyclical ignorance and retribution lies on both the offender and the offended for not knowing or not caring about the following:

- ➢ Personal identity and value.
- ➢ Unconditional regard for other people.
- ➢ Appropriate ways to express one's self verbally and emotionally.
- ➢ When to challenge and when to keep quiet.
- ➢ "It's not just *what* one says, but *how* it is said!"
- ➢ Who deserves one's energy.
- ➢ The positive or negative influences one possesses.
- ➢ Destructive ways one projects unsolicited views that are personal issues.
- ➢ The lasting impressions and impacts one makes on others with words and actions (or omittance of them).
- ➢ Constructive ways to protect one's self from another person's unwarranted personal issues.
- ➢ How to walk in other people's shoes.

It is easier to handle people who do not know any better. As long as they are willing to be enlightened and change, then half the battle is won. It is entirely different when they are just flat out unwilling to learn or change. I guess unwilling people are here for lessons in life. They teach us what not to do, as well as sharpen our skills to live **UNAPOLOGETICALLY**. They are like that concept of sand and debris that polishes a jewel into existence. Walking in other people's shoes, whether in conversation, actions, or mentally, is one of many key factors to living the **UNAPOLOGETIC** life. Most times, we receive the same measure of grace, mercy, and tolerance we often give. Those who do not deserve it need a little more.

[14]

As we take the blinders off our eyes, we see a clearer picture of our personal conditions, as well as the condition of our ecosystem. We also gain insight into other people's worlds and find common grounds. We can choose to create peace in our differences. That sounds so simple, but perhaps we just need to be reminded. Do you agree we need to make a change in our society? I surely do. Here is the purpose of my personal commitment to make a difference wherever I go.

Chapter Three

UNAPOLOGETICALLY COMMISSIONED

This "commission" came into fruition because I have naturally gray hair—a double no-no in society's beauty handbook. According to their outdated handbook, my hair is supposed to be straightened with no signs of kinkiness or gray. Fortunately, the natural hair movement is becoming more prevalent. Unfortunately, the struggle is still very real for mature women with gray hair or for those like me who grayed prematurely.

I am watching younger women dye their hair gray or add in gray extensions. Inexplicably, it is mostly older women and a few older men who question me with disdain about my gray hair. Some women tell me about their wish to wear their gray hair but have all kinds of reasons why they cannot or will not. In my personal opinion, this makes me very sad. How awesome would the following scenario be? Witnessing more of the older generations setting examples on how to age naturally with a coveted attractiveness in grace and dignity while being true to themselves and their appearances! We can be stylish and full of vitality with gray hair and wrinkles!

I actually like that the younger people are wearing gray hair, even if it may be a fad. They are on to something that most of their elders are not. The younger ones are demonstrating the position the elders could take: "Gray hair should be worn with confidence and attitude. Gray does not age you. You age yourself!" I have been told numerous times that I do not look my age for one whose head is almost covered with all white hair. This often causes major confusion, but I will not be sorry for my natural life progression colliding with my good self-care. This is my true essence of living **UNAPOLOGETICALLY** gray!

A significant portion of my purpose is to facilitate your journey to your **UNAPOLOGETIC** life. I want to inspire a movement for those who are discriminated against because of their looks when there is so much more inside of them. It is time out for retreating, retaliating, or conforming out of fear, hurt, and shame. I desire to see people band together within to create a safe place for healing and unity among families, communities, cross-culturally, and, ultimately, our nation. There are no "members-only club" mentalities because exclusion is not necessary. People are either going to get right or get gone on their own accord.

We use our journeys to edify others. We do not share our battles for pity. The purposes of our battles are to advocate and seek justice against ignorance with the greatest intelligence and impact. This is our chance to share the greatness we possess beyond what people see. We will not be sorry for what we look like because of who we are, how we were born or developed into. We choose not to exist like porcupines in danger, which will not let anything get too close. A porcupine's protective quills—much like our personas, words, and actions—will either repel or damage anything that comes in close proximity to them. We need each other. Most of all, we motivate others to live out their **UNAPOLOGETIC** lives boldly. The supreme goal is to live and let others live as we discover and appreciate the diversity of our society. It starts with us accepting and confidently walking out who we are as individuals first. We intentionally make a positive contribution to a society that can sometimes be superficial, selfish, and heartless.

Are you ready to live **UNAPOLOGETICALLY** in your skin? Are you prepared to wake up and recognize some stuff?

Chapter Four

WHERE'S THE LOVE?

It is a sad time when we are getting further and further away from our authentic selves. We have given people the unauthorized power to declare what is normal or "the look," and that particular standard is considered "the way" for everybody. These strange voices prey upon those who are already down on themselves. Disheartened souls follow these beguiling voices like sheep that are led into strange territories where even _they_ know they don't belong. We are also wandering aimlessly into a depersonalized era where embracing what is unnatural over what is natural is no big deal, especially in beauty standards.

My heart goes out to so many people, especially women, who have fallen victims to this debauchery. We strive too hard for approval and acceptance, only to fall flat on our faces against some cold, hard realities. Many are starting to see the damaging effects, untold amounts of money spent, and wasted time and energy from consistently trying to maintain a standard for a world that has not always been kind to us.

Discrimination on any level due to pure ignorance or blatant hatred adds salt to our wounds, all because "they" do not like who we are and how we look...and neither do we.

Most of all, we have not been kind to ourselves. Our unkindness is evident in our self-talk about how bad we are or look. We act it out in our decisions to cover up, get rid of certain things, or assume powerlessness before we attempt anything. It is even more heartbreaking when children adopt self-defeating monologues that were started by adults! Someone or something fed us some mess, and we took it as the truth. When we put toxic words in the atmosphere about ourselves, we often wonder why we experience conflicts in various parts of our lives! Even though our bodies charge forward on autopilot, our inner selves often revolt or shut down.

Everything around us reflects our internal state. You know the saying, "A house divided will surely fall"? Well, the most obvious signs are wavering in decision-making, unforeseen reasons why doors slam in our faces, and unstable relationships. Those are just a few scenarios that can result when we have personal strife from within. When there is "oneness" within our triune beings (bodies, minds, and spirits), our confidence soars. We have a successful Law of Attraction working on our side. Can we take a moment to pull ourselves together in love?

Here is more food for thought just for you: If you cannot love yourself unconditionally with what you and the world claim are your flaws, why should you expect someone to work harder at loving you more than you love yourself? It is challenging to love people who do not love themselves. It seems inconceivable to know how to receive pure love or anything else most times for those who struggle with loving themselves. Feelings of unworthiness and unintentional rejection of anything of value frequently occurs without self-love.

Life is hard when you don't like you. Living **UNAPOLOGETICALLY** will be off-kilter to you. You will use **UNAPOLOGETIC** moments like a hermit's shell, an inexperienced numb-chucks user, or drop them and run every time you get hit with undesirable treatments. There is good news, though! All hope is not lost! Let's see how we can turn this around for your good, shall we? Let's do a checkup and look at your reflections.

CHECKUP TIME

Let's assess where you are right now. Reflect on the total sum of who you are, what you look like, how you were born, or developed into. What unpleasant things do you or others bring to light? How does your self-talk, thoughts, and treatment of yourself truthfully rank on a scale of 1-5?

- ➢ 1 = I need an intervention, hands down.
- ➢ 2 = I am in a tunnel and see the light, but it is not a train.
- ➢ 3 = I am on the fence but leaning towards the hopeful side.
- ➢ 4 = I am not perfect, but I am strong enough to grow in treating myself better.
- ➢ 5 = I am pretty good to myself.

Sit on your number for a moment and really feel it. Ponder your state intensely. Feel it to the point that you are contemplating some alternative decisions, if necessary. Depending on where you are, and if you want to see change, your final move is to take one of three actions:

1. Seek professional or spiritual help immediately to work through past or current hurts and fears;
2. Move forward with changing old beliefs and behaviors to replace them with healthier thoughts and habits; or,
3. Enjoy this book and use it to help someone else who is struggling.

Any of these choices are doable. It is time to be **UNAPOLOGETIC** in your skin. Let's clear your space and move forward.

Keep in mind: This is about what the world identifies as your unlikeable features to the point that it has you feeling some type of way about yourself based on your appearance. Please understand this is not to cause you to dwell on your past. It has nothing to do with what you did or did not do. Neither is it about what someone is doing or has done to you. You know the hamster wheel on which you tread. What they said or didn't say. What they did or didn't do. You have identified every imaginable wrong thing that you and everyone have done for a long time now. You have beaten that proverbial dead horse too many times. It is dead and nasty. What is even grosser is when you carry that dead horse on your back, in your head, and within your heart. I am also willing to bet that you make yourself sick with it, including your sphere of influence.

There is no such thing as pleasing ignorant people who have no valid reason to dislike you! For what reasons should conflict and abuse from the malicious views of others have the right to dwell within you? You are so much more than what people are trying to focus on! Do you agree it is time for a change? You can choose the freedom to live an **UNAPOLOGETIC** life in peace and harmony with yourself first and then with others. If you are ready to move on, let's face the internal war and answer the following questions right now:

It's Time for a Change!

*Write about who you would be if the negativity was not taking up space in your mind. How would you be? (This has nothing to do with changing your looks or predicting other people's actions. This is **ALL** about who and how you would realistically be without perceived limitations.) Read it several times. Is it positive and doable? Go back to the drawing board, if necessary.*

_____

_____

_____

_____

_____

_____

_____

_____

_____

_____

_____

_____

_____

_____

_____

_____

_____

_____

_____

_____

_____

What can you do to identify the triggers that snatch you into a downward spiral of self-loathing and blaming? Do the triggers occur from what you think or do? Is it something provoked through your five senses? What about your affiliations or locations?

_____

_____

_____

_____

_____

_____

_____

_____

_____

_____

_____

_____

_____

_____

_____

_____

_____

_____

_____

_____

_____

_____

_____

_____

_____

_____

In what ways can you immediately stop the triggers and get back on track?

_____

_____

_____

_____

_____

_____

_____

_____

_____

_____

_____

_____

_____

_____

_____

_____

_____

_____

_____

_____

_____

_____

_____

_____

_____

_____

_____

_____

What methods can you use to create positive thoughts and habits for yourself?

_____

_____

_____

_____

_____

_____

_____

_____

_____

_____

_____

_____

_____

_____

_____

_____

_____

_____

_____

_____

_____

_____

_____

_____

_____

_____

_____

_____

Who is your accountability person(s) to share your methods with as you complete your inner work?

_____

_____

_____

_____

_____

_____

_____

_____

_____

_____

_____

_____

_____

_____

_____

_____

_____

_____

_____

_____

_____

_____

_____

_____

_____

_____

Chapter Five

TRUE REFLECTION REVELATION

This reflection revelation has nothing to do with your outer appearance. Unhook yourself from the obvious for a moment. What does the "inner" you look or sound like? Let me introduce you to him or her.

It is the most truthful part of you that exists when everything within, on, and around you are facades. It is the part of you that is real, swells, lights up, applauds, and has a constructive voice when you proactively take a protective stance to be your authentic self. It is also that part of you that cringes, cries, rages, or shuts down whenever you or someone says something insensitive about you.

Some of you may think this next part is corny, and that is okay. This is your cue to skip the next two paragraphs...but why would you?

There are far too many people who look like they have it all together, but they are either brutally battered on the inside or have been shackled and silenced indefinitely. This may be the moment of truth that some people have not faced in years or not at all. Some of you may prefer a healthy, trusted confidant to talk you through this process. When is the last time you just sat silently before yourself in the mirror for a long time with your perceived flaws and an open mind? This really is for you if you are experiencing resistance for any reason. Are you willing to silence all distractions in your head and around you so that you can face the most magnificent image and gift known to mankind?

Spend some time with yourself in the mirror quietly and stare into the eyes of your own soul. This is not the time to rush, ridicule or doubt the process, criticize yourself, or turn away. In the following section, take notes of what you are hearing, as well as what you are feeling overall. Use this time also to take inventory of all the things you have been telling yourself about you. Do not bring other people and situations into this moment. This is all about you, and no one else. Can you turn off the mental sewer pipeline for a moment? It is time to become one with your inner person by honoring the good you hear and see. Once you are truly tuned in to the essence of you, I am curious to know, what is (s)he telling you?

➢ Is s(he) telling you that you have been lied to too long and it is time to let your natural state shine because you truly are attractive?

➢ Is s(he) regurgitating on you all the abusive tapes you constantly replay as truth?

> ➢ Is s(he) saying that you are wasting too much money, time, resources, or space trying to keep up something that no one is really impressed with or paying attention to anyway?
> ➢ Is s(he) saying that your health—whether spiritually, physically, mentally, emotionally, or financially—is at stake and you need to make some changes?

What do you do for yourself now? Do you need to apologize? Forgive? Reprogram destructive talk with constructive truths? Let go or cut off? Dig deeper? Heal? Love? Get educated? Do more or less of receiving or giving? Take a risk? Shine more? *Take some type of action to start or stop? What else? Are you getting directions to help you move forward?

---

*Disclaimer: Take actions that are not illegal, intrusive, abusive, or immoral to yourself and others. Don't even try it. Pleading insanity rarely gets you off the hook. Some issues you may be challenged with are usually deeper than what is seen or felt. The truth of the matter is that what is going on within reflects on the outside, even if you cannot readily identify what it is. The purpose of this exercise is to expose what has been buried within. If you get stuck or this process becomes too painful for you, I strongly recommend you please seek professional help immediately.

SELF-REFLECTION NOTES

_____
_____
_____
_____
_____
_____
_____
_____
_____
_____
_____
_____
_____
_____
_____
_____
_____
_____
_____
_____
_____
_____
_____
_____
_____
_____
_____

You may have just received a revelation of what hinders you from being **UNAPOLOGETICALLY** you!

I challenge you to make this time alone with yourself in silence a frequent practice. After a short period of time, the mirror will no longer be needed because you know what to expect. I use this exercise as a personal practice regularly to get in tune with myself about life. I truly appreciate the results! When the reflection exercise is done with an expectation for answers and change, insight and healing may perhaps evolve into a move towards strengthening your inner core in an **UNAPOLOGETIC** life.

Take advantage of opportunities to get centered and check in with yourself. It is time to silence the voices speaking into our lives, which cause us distraction or immunity to the chatter. Our discernment needs fine-tuning to differentiate our conditions that are sometimes crying out but cannot be heard past the voices. Can you imagine the good you deserve beyond the constant ostracizing and criticizing from yourself and others? Who would not put a person in their place quickly for talking disrespectfully to or about someone they love? However, people allow themselves to be mistreated. Most of all, they are the worst abusers of themselves. Predator personalities love to devour victim personalities.

Let me gently remind you that you cannot control what others do. You can, however, control how you respond and what you do. You have all the insight you need pertaining to you and your life. Remember that you are here to be celebrated—not simply tolerated or berated.

First thing's first: Stop being a predator against yourself. It is time to protect and nurture you. What boundaries could you set for yourself internally? Ideas of those boundaries might include knowing who or what provokes your negative emotions and responses, proactively learning how to express yourself appropriately, and deciding who deserves your energy. What about boundaries for others? Boundaries for others might include silence to stupid comments, calmly nipping foolish behavior in the bud in the right timing, and diplomatically setting the tone for what you will or won't tolerate with consequences you deliberately follow through on. You know what works best for your personality and the atmosphere you are in. Consider all angles and choose wisely.

Tuning in to the Essence of You

This is your safe space. Plan to spend a long time in silence with no distractions in front of a mirror. A trusted friend with a healthy attitude can serve as a sounding board. If possible, do it in your natural state without whatever you normally cover up with. Be mindful and takes notes of whatever comes to your mind.

_____

_____

_____

_____

_____

_____

_____

_____

_____

_____

_____

_____

_____

_____

_____

_____

_____

_____

_____

_____

_____

_____

_____

_____

Is it necessary to seek professional help or are you able to move forward to make healthy choices for yourself? Explain your choice.

_____

_____

_____

_____

_____

_____

_____

_____

_____

_____

_____

_____

_____

_____

_____

_____

_____

_____

_____

_____

_____

_____

_____

_____

_____

_____

_____

What do you want to see changed that can help you accept yourself as you are?

_____

_____

_____

_____

_____

_____

_____

_____

_____

_____

_____

_____

_____

_____

_____

_____

_____

_____

_____

_____

_____

_____

_____

_____

_____

_____

_____

How do you plan to make changes that will bring healing and strength to you?

_____

_____

_____

_____

_____

_____

_____

_____

_____

_____

_____

_____

_____

_____

_____

_____

_____

_____

_____

_____

_____

_____

_____

_____

_____

_____

_____

_____

_____

Is there a healthy accountability person or mentor to assist you? Write that name here and describe the qualities that make that person your ideal candidate. If you are without a candidate presently, write your desired needs that person should possess.

_____

_____

_____

_____

_____

_____

_____

_____

_____

_____

_____

_____

_____

_____

_____

_____

_____

_____

_____

_____

_____

_____

_____

_____

_____

_____

_____

What healthy boundaries can you establish for yourself and others?

Without focusing on what you __do__, look at your internal characteristics and list your strengths.

_____

_____

_____

_____

_____

_____

_____

_____

_____

_____

_____

_____

_____

_____

_____

_____

_____

_____

_____

_____

_____

_____

_____

_____

_____

_____

_____

_____

_____

Chapter Six

MY PERSONAL REFLECTION REVELATION

I started seeing gray hairs as a teen; however, my transition accelerated in my mid to late '40s. There was an 8-year span when a combination of premature graying genes and a continuously stressful life expedited the graying of my hair. I started hearing comments of distaste about my hair turning white and the "need to do something because you are too young for all that gray." I was experiencing major vulnerability due to the low-blow combination of circumstances beyond my control and consequences of my poor choices. I had to choose between living or looks.

Dying my hair by myself was out of the question. With hair that grows fast and an overly-sensitive scalp, I could not see myself scraping up $80-$100 I did not have every 2 to 4 weeks to ensure my hair would be done professionally when I needed to survive. None of my critics were offering to pay to get my hair done.

[42]

While stewing in my hurt feelings one day in front of the mirror, the thought occurred to me: "Everybody's got something to say, but they know I'm not in a position to do anything about it. No one's taking me to get my hair fixed, either. This gray is not bothering me anyway. All my life, I've always jumped to the tune of someone saying, 'You would look better if you…' and what all I could do or stop doing to be more liked. Where are these people in my life now? Nowhere!" Yes, that was the 12-year-old girl in my grown-up body who finally got tired and had more sense than the adult in me. She came out swinging that day!

On that pivotal day in the mirror, my caveat became, "This is me. If a man cannot appreciate me in my natural state now, he never will. If it becomes impossible to get my hair dyed for any reason, this is what he will be waking up to every day. It's better that he likes me as I am now." During my process of becoming **UNAPOLOGETICALLY** gray, I first learned I needed to be honest with myself about appreciating me instead of making my priority be all about people. I am a low-maintenance woman by nature. Unfortunately, I found myself internally caving at the criticisms of what others thought about my hair. My growth happened when I concentrated on learning more about who I was, coupled with the dire need of taking responsibility to nurture myself. I had doctored up the external me for too long. My work had to happen from the inside out.

My self-prescribed treatment consisted of healing for my wounded heart by strengthening my spiritual life and rediscovering my worth. My spirit and soul were the most

[43]

important parts to focus on because they are the true essence of me. Both needed to be on one accord and healthy since they rule my body! A more profound presence of love and light flourished within me, and it remains. With that presence came wisdom and authority. People can be as presumptuous as they want, but I strive to mentally dispel their entitlement to freedom of speech from affecting me. I write the script of my life, not them! In my script, my gray became my tiara because I am royalty. I carried myself like the gentle queen I was predestined to be.

There is something so powerful about getting a revelation of something wonderful to come, writing and reciting your vision, and carrying yourself as if it is already so. Call it hocus-pocus if you want to, but I am living proof of it! I acquired the much-needed confidence to enlighten, ignore, or silence my critics and the curious.

You now have the general scoop of how my reflection revelation helped me to become rooted in my **UNAPOLOGETICALLY** gray life. Your paths will be different than mine, but let's see what direction you will take with yours, shall we?

Chapter Seven

A SOLID CENTER:
YOUR WHO, WHAT, AND HOW

What strengths — particularly your inherent characteristics — do you have to focus on about who you are versus what you do? People will do their best to cancel you out, no matter what you do or how hard you try. Rejection sucks. You better have some internal worth to capitalize on to keep you strong!

Which one of the following helps you stand in the face of opposition? Do you have a wall for blocking all access, a hedge of thorns to strike back, a lack of established boundaries, or do you have a solid center to command an atmosphere of dignity for everyone while being **UNAPOLOGETICALLY** you?

What does "possessing a solid center in the face of opposition" mean to you?

[45]

What does "command an atmosphere of dignity for everyone" mean to you?

What happens? How must you be or not be?

Pen your truths here.

_____

_____

_____

_____

_____

_____

_____

_____

_____

_____

_____

_____

_____

_____

_____

_____

_____

_____

_____

_____

_____

_____

_____

_____

_____

Your honest answers may provide some direction for the necessary mindset and protective changes or for you to keep doing what you do in the face of critics. Put your answers aside for a moment for comparison later.

It is very difficult to live an **UNAPOLOGETIC** life if you do not have a strong foundation about who you are, why you are, and how you are. These are the building blocks of your solid center. If you were not programmed with a strong sense of identity and prepared to face a world that may not accept you as you are, people will define you in ways you were never meant to be. You will step to every pace presented to please people, or you will be combative with your own shadow and others while forging your identity. In either position, people will try to label you or fill you with mess that does not fit. You may be in this predicament right now or know someone who is. I get the pleasure of sparking your thought process to make a change for the better! I believe in you enough to know that you do have the answers.

Please allow me to briefly share my personal inner work with you that helped strengthen my core to be **UNAPOLOGETIC**.

I learned that a solid center about myself was necessary kind of late in life. My perception about my worth was very weak, so people-pleasing took precedence over self-preservation clear into adulthood. Once I learned some particulars about the who, why, and how of my make-up and confirmed what I knew about myself, I truly began to understand my worth and purpose.

Here are some things I discovered, as well as established, about myself:

- ➤ **Who I am?** First of all, I am chosen. Being chosen is unique to me because it is not a role I fulfill or something I do, but it sure enhances everything about me and my destiny. Of course, there is the obvious. I am a daughter, wife, mother, sister, family member, and businesswoman. I am an influential woman who inspires others to choose healthier lifestyles. I am a coach who empowers others to be successful in various areas of their lives. I provide ministry moments to individuals who need it.

- ➤ **Next: Why I am?** I was victimized as a child. The consequences of that, plus more violations in my youth and adult life, caused me to lose my voice and power. Although I am still very soft-spoken, I do have a strong expression to declare liberty and the power to act for myself and others. I no longer allow people to define me the way they see fit. My traits and roles were tattooed in my DNA to lead, be resilient, nurture, inspire, counsel or coach, and empower. These were clearly evident throughout my transitions from the bossy 2-year-old to the wounded 12-year-old, shapeless, boney, short-haired girl who hung in there to fully rebound. Now, I am a powerful, mature, gray-haired woman who facilitates healthy change for others.

- ➤ **Lastly: How I am?** I may not be perfect, but I am dynamic in my growth right before your eyes. I am secure in who I am and how I look. I am protective of my rights and the rights of others who are discriminated against. I endeavor to use the least combative ways to initially deal with ignorance. I want my messages (not just my emotions) to be heard, except when it is appropriate to respond in ways that only foolish or compassionate people can understand.

All of this was learned in quiet time with myself and God (you can choose to be with your higher power or yourself). I conscientiously answered deeply evocative questions from other sources that made me think hard about my worth, values, and principles. I was constantly challenged to reframe how I could realistically see myself in a better state than in my current situation. My reframed situations were turned into declarations that I still recite daily and can change as needed. I carefully observed those who modeled the appropriate responses in moments of disagreements that left everyone with dignity. This is why the work is from the inside out and has nothing to do with outer appearances. You know the deal. What is happening on the inside manifests on the outside.

Now, it is your turn. I challenge you to consider the following elements about yourself:

➤ Your make-up (i.e., history, familial influence on you, temperament, etc.).
➤ Your weak points where people will hit you and cause you to "crumble" or "lose it."
➤ Your strengths that get you noticed from who you are and how you are (character traits).

Your Who, What, and How Notes

_____
_____
_____
_____
_____
_____
_____
_____
_____
_____
_____
_____
_____
_____
_____
_____
_____
_____
_____
_____
_____
_____
_____
_____
_____
_____
_____
_____
_____
_____

Reflect on the conduct that has brought about negative or positive results for you. What has been working for you or not working for you? If you are not for sure, ask your sphere of influence. Do not shy away or become defensive to what you learn. Mindset renewal is a great tool for an **UNAPOLOGETIC** life. This is your opportunity to strengthen your foundation so that your center will be solid when storms come. You want to be rooted securely in your position and emotions in the midst of discrimination and rejection.

Knowing what you are made of and how you were created to function are vital to prevailing over ignorance. Yes, you will have some raw emotions, but what you do with them reveals how strongly you are anchored. No one causes you to drift from anything that is destined for you when you know this. Erase the negative internal tapes and routines by mentally or verbally rehearsing where you want your life to go. Say what you want; not just what you *do not* want. These practices are beneficial habits to possess on a daily basis. Your thoughts and words majorly influence the direction of your life.

You *ARE* worthy of being treated with respect and receiving what is rightfully yours. I think that is a good daily meditation mantra right there as a reminder when you are in the storm of social adversity. People are watching.

Recalibrating Your Center

If you are not sure that you have a solid center to command an atmosphere of dignity in conflict, how would you conduct yourself on a good day? What is your immediate action? How are your emotions during this time? What does your naysayer look like when you address them? How do you feel afterwards?

_____

_____

_____

_____

_____

_____

_____

_____

_____

_____

_____

_____

_____

_____

_____

_____

_____

_____

_____

_____

_____

What about the true test when you encounter senselessness people and situations on a bad day? What is your immediate action? How are your emotions during this time? What does your naysayer look like when you address them? How do you feel afterwards?

_____

_____

_____

_____

_____

_____

_____

_____

_____

_____

_____

_____

_____

_____

_____

_____

_____

_____

_____

_____

_____

_____

_____

_____

_____

_____

Reflect on the bullet points about the elements of you to determine what has or has not been working for you. Take into consideration your conduct, attitudes, habits, particular traits, and manners. Most of all, be aware of your communication. Is there a difference between what you want to be and do versus who you are and what you do?

_____

_____

_____

_____

_____

_____

_____

_____

_____

_____

_____

_____

_____

_____

_____

_____

_____

_____

_____

_____

_____

_____

_____

_____

_____

What is necessary for you to change or keep doing what you are doing?

_____

_____

_____

_____

_____

_____

_____

_____

_____

_____

_____

_____

_____

_____

_____

_____

_____

_____

_____

_____

_____

_____

_____

_____

_____

_____

_____

_____

_____

What are appropriate methods to renew your mind with better thoughts and actions?

_____

_____

_____

_____

_____

_____

_____

_____

_____

_____

_____

_____

_____

_____

_____

_____

_____

_____

_____

_____

_____

_____

_____

_____

_____

_____

_____

Chapter Eight

PREDATOR AND VICTIM PERSONALITIES

B e mindful that people are studying you or believe they already have you figured out. Remember those predator and victim personalities I mentioned earlier? Look at yourself with brutal honesty in the following personalities to see where you fit. Don't be trying to identify others, either! This is solely about you and trust me; this will not be easy.

Victims cry out and bleed from their current scars and old wounds. Victims are sometimes irresponsible as they tell their stories to anyone in hopes that somebody will rescue or protect them. Victims seek attention by any means necessary or by default when they are self-negligent.

Predators are looking for someone to dominate and devour. Predators are shrewdly calculating as they wait for a sign of weakness to attack. Alpha predators also look for other predators to defeat so they can remain in control. Predators smell a victim perpetrating as another predator a mile away — bloody!

Being a victim is never a good thing, no matter how much attention and benevolence is bestowed. Helplessness potentially opens the door to subconsciously teaching others how to devalue victims. Predators gladly take advantage of the vulnerable. Seasoned victims eventually evolve into manipulators who are definitely low-key predators.

On the other hand, being a predator is never a good thing, either. Predators are always looking for someone or something to conquer or control. Who can trust a predator? Ruthlessness eclipses any good intentions.

If you find yourself leaning towards the predator personality, you have probably been wronged more times than you care to admit. You, too, are a victim and deserve healing as well.

Don't like what you observed about yourself? Get the proper help you deserve so that you will have a stronger, solid center, whether it is through spiritual counseling or therapy, taking courses on conflict management or assertiveness, joining a support group to practice self-confidence, or whatever activities that will work best for you.

Let's get a different perspective from serpents and doves to see if it can help with your **UNAPOLOGETIC** lifestyle.

UNAPOLOGETIC Nuggets

*If you were brutally honest with yourself and could identify traits from either side, I want to acknowledge your hard work! That was not an easy task. I had to partake of this exercise, and it was not easy for me, either! If it makes you feel any better, I found traits to work on, too. The master keys for unlocking ties from either personality trait is to forgive and let go of people, places, and things that keep you bound to the memories and pain. Do not feel bad if you cannot do this on your own. Drop your pride and get some help so you can be **UNAPOLOGETICALLY** free!*

*Victim or Predator? Who am I? Why Am I? How am I? What am I willing to do to become **UNAPOLOGETICALLY** free?*

_____

_____

_____

_____

_____

_____

_____

_____

_____

_____

_____

_____

_____

_____

_____

_____

_____

_____

_____

_____

_____

_____

_____

_____

_____

_____

_____

Chapter Nine

THE SERPENT AND THE DOVE: THE PERFECT BLEND

You might not be religious at all, so you may not think this part applies to you. Wrong! Granted, the portion of text referenced is regarding the disciples carrying the Gospel, but you all have something in common. This timeless principle also applies to your everyday conduct because guess what? Your life is a message, regardless if you think it is private or public and whether it is the good news or the bad news. People are watching, reading, studying, and defining you in their minds as you are on your daily mission. Check this out to see just how beneficial this principle really is to you.

In His wisdom, Jesus sent the disciples on an assignment with a specific warning: He said He was sending them out as sheep among wolves, but He told them to be wise as serpents and harmless as doves (Matthew 10:16). Unkind people, like wolves, travel in packs to gang up on whomever they feel are threatening, weak, or misfits. The disciples were peculiar men

[61]

who did some mind-blowing stuff! People did not like them, what they stood for, or what they did. Jesus' cautionary analogy prepared them on how to be vigilantly **UNAPOLOGETIC** about their mission and lives. The disciples had to be confident in their greatness without being obnoxious or drawing negative attention to themselves.

There is nothing new under the sun. Nowadays, not only does one's religious status bring marginalization and persecution, but what that person looks like, where a person was born, how that person was born, and even one's stage of life may create the same risk. In essence, we were also sent into this increasingly predominant wolf-like, predator society as sheep who may or may not be prepared to survive. Unfortunately, this includes some families, neighborhoods, schools, jobs, cities, etc.

Are you equipped to handle someone who does not like you, how you look or your life's message? What about people who want to make you disappear? Are you that predator who wants to make people disappear and desires to change? Pay attention! How do people carry out both characteristics of two polar opposite creatures? What is so special about serpents and doves?

Serpents and doves are very similar in that fact that they:

➢ Are fascinating to watch because they are pretty and have human-like traits.
➢ Have discernment to know when dangerous situations are imminent.
➢ Know how to escape quickly.

> ➢ Are peaceful creatures, as long as they are not disturbed.

Here are where the major differences come in.

Serpents are very wise, calculating, and ultra-sensitive to their surroundings. They scurry when they sense danger and find various places of safety quickly. They definitely have predator instincts for protection and survival. They are not afraid to strike when they feel endangered, but their first choice is usually to get away.

In contrast, doves are very gentle and peaceful. They also sense danger and take flight far above it to remove themselves. Even when they are defensive, they will not maim or kill you. Doves do not have predator instincts like serpents, which makes them innocent.

Can you see how valuable it would be to blend the strengths of the serpent and the dove? What a less dysfunctional world this would be if everyone strived to have a good balance of these two traits! Unfortunately, inconsiderate people are just as necessary as respectful people to make the world function.

Meditate on this: What would your life be like if you were in a chilled state around people, regardless of what they believe about you? You know you are among callous or ultra-inquisitive people, but you maintain your gentle state. They are reading you or presume they already know something about you. They may assume you are threatening like a serpent, dangerous like other wolves, powerless like a dove, or even simple-minded like sheep. Remember: They have sized you up by your appearance or put you in a stereotypical category.

When you have reached a place of personal strength and understanding, it is incredible what you see. You are sensitive to your environment. You are discerning them carefully. If motives are not right towards you, you are not caught off guard. You do not have to be provoked because you clearly see through your adversaries. You see them for who they are, what they stand for, and what they do. You might even be able to anticipate the actions of those you are dealing with. As a matter of fact, you have already calculated your next move. If the atmosphere is not right, you peacefully make your decision to educate, walk away, or legitimately strike back to make them back up off you (yes, I meant that). Depending on how much venom you release, you can either poison or kill them. Unless you are truly in survival mode, you have defeated the purpose of the **UNAPOLOGETIC** way if you harm them. You stooped to their disgraceful level with your excessive toxins. If you used the right amount of venom, you stun them in a way they won't forget, but they are not crippled. They leave you alone and possibly respect you, too.

This scenario of the well-blended serpent and dove qualities are the essence of operating in an **UNAPOLOGETIC** culture. You have the global mindset that you and all that pertains to you are worth making wise decisions. Your decisions significantly impact your future and those associated with you.

UNAPOLOGETIC Nuggets

*Notice that this has nothing to do with being passive and taking abuse from anyone or anything. The **UNAPOLOGETIC** code of conduct is never to be offensive. You choose your rightful intensity of defense when the need arises. You make the decision to remain in control and not let someone initiate the cause of you being out of control. Success of the code of conduct consists of you knowing your value.*

Refer back to your notes in "A Solid Center: Your Who, What, and How" to see if any adjustments need to be made regarding your solid center to command an atmosphere of dignity for everyone.

The Serpent and Dove Blend: How I Can Make it Work for Me

Chapter Ten

BEING RESPONSIBLY UNAPOLOGETIC

Your proper mindset and attitude are crucial because your presentation is a deal-maker or deal-breaker for the **UNAPOLOGETIC** culture. If you are going to represent, please do it right! There are too many people being so negatively unapologetic. A positive **UNAPOLOGETIC** life is demonstrated by the assurance of your worth in a way that is healthy for you but leaves your critics with a show of face. In other words, you are assertive without ripping someone's face or head off, even if they deserve it. They need their face and head to comprehend the magnitude of what you said or did. Without their face and head that you just figuratively lopped off, they cannot see, hear, or think about anything you did or said. For real, though! All of your energy was in vain, and they really did not hear your heart. You may have been just the right person to help them learn and apply wisdom.

People need to experience the best side of you that they wrongly imagined never existed. If you do not care what people think about you, control yourself accordingly for the sake of the rest of the group. Rest of what group, you ask? The group you represent that offenders already hold negatively in their minds. Stand anchored maturely with your tactful position in the face of conflict, even if you do not feel it. Be sure to find constructive ways and outlets to express your destructive thoughts and actions. You have to get the poison out and off of you. Safeguard your outlets so they do not include people, places, or things that will incite your motivation towards destruction. This is ultimately to your benefit. If not, your pent-up hurt and anger will become cracks in your foundation. As you know, cracks eventually cause you to crumble or blow up...and lose it.

UNAPOLOGETIC Nuggets

*I know, I know! What other people think about you or us really should not matter. However, in the grand scheme of things, we have a dual responsibility to the **UNAPOLOGETIC** culture. We must be true to ourselves, yet guard the face of whatever group we represent in the minds of ignorant people. We strive to leave no room for critics to clap back at us. I recognize that sometimes, it might be an impossible task to be peaceful, depending on whom you are dealing with. Just do your best to represent us all well. They will get their justified consequence based on your appropriate response.*

Your feelings do matter, so find a healthy manner to take care of yourself after any social mishaps. Don't sweep them under the rug. Deal with them in a responsible way. Stay out of the victim and predator traps! Please!

Refer back to your notes in "A Solid Center: Your Who, What, and How" to see if any adjustments need to be made regarding your solid center to command an atmosphere of dignity for everyone.

Ways to adjust my solid center to become responsibly **UNAPOLOGETIC**.

_____

_____

_____

_____

_____

_____

_____

_____

_____

_____

_____

_____

_____

_____

_____

_____

_____

_____

_____

_____

_____

_____

_____

_____

_____

Chapter Eleven

DON'T BE SORRY, BE LEGITIMATELY UNAPOLOGETIC

It is critical to work through maladaptive thoughts, behaviors, or anything that prompts you to either implode or explode. In living the **UNAPOLOGETIC** life, you cannot internalize the ugliness, nor react with anything to be sorry for later. When people are very curious or hateful, and it requires a response, confidently communicate or tactfully disarm them with what you want them to know. For some people, silence is golden! Not everyone or everything deserves the privilege of a response from you. You get the chance to model what it means to bridle the tongue to those with broken oral filters. Silence gives them and others an opportunity to hear how they really sound without the fuel of your participation. They are not only forced to sit in their verbal sewage, but they look unintelligent, too. Only fools can have a one-sided argument or a verbally abusive monologue by themselves.

I love the biblical proverbs that advise us not to even **answer** foolish people when they are speaking recklessly. Now, that requires discipline like no other! You set the tone for creating an environment where your tact or silence reveals to people that they really should think twice before speaking. Know that your response (or lack of) is the critical factor in the exchange.

Your ultimate goal is to communicate your message, not necessarily your emotions or anything else. Your impression is accomplished verbally or nonverbally. Ask yourself: Are my precious emotions and energies truly worth detonating on ignorance? A resounding "YES!" should be reserved for the protection of rights and against any malicious attacks. Be careful of what you do and how you do it, though! More than likely, there are those who probably expect you to get on their level and go completely bad on them. As a matter of fact, there are some who intend to purposely provoke you. They want to prove their stereotypical hypothesis right, cause a scene, start a fight, and worse, bait you into legal trouble or take your life. Taking your life may not necessarily mean death, either. Protect your freedom and rights. As my grandmother used to say, "There are worse things than death." Center yourself and disarm them with the unexpected. Practice that good old fashion, "Pass the salt and pepper, please?" voice tone when you address your cynics. Go on! Say it over and over again. Use it whenever you get angry. People cannot hear you when you are screaming and yelling anyway. No, really! They hear your loud voice with all of the posturing, foul language, and emotions, but they cannot hear anything else you say. Be mindful of what you want to communicate as well as your transmission of it. Take some time to consider what to do or say that makes people think, apologize, agree, or perhaps respectfully disagree with you. Influencing reactions with your responses is an acquired skill that must be done with precision and authenticity. Your tone, choice of words, and body language mean everything! You have already experienced enough off the wall remarks and treatments to create your own personal artillery of next responses, or you can just walk away.

I grew weary of being embarrassed by not responding appropriately to stupid remarks or very curious people. My reactions often resulted in astonishment, hurt, and frustration. It took work to put my emotions back together after I gave someone a piece of my mind for their unsolicited comments. I still have to catch myself at times and remember that my mind is too precious to waste on foolishness. I know I am preaching to the choir right now. This is for the author, too. How are we supposed to handle ourselves in the heat of the moment?

UNAPOLOGETIC Nuggets

When you are self-assured about who you are and why you are, there is nothing more stinging to cynics than a confident look with no response. Remember: Silence speaks volumes!

Demonstration of too much disgust indicates that the hater's mission of provoking or shaming you was accomplished. A look of disgust only works well when you do it with a cool measure of nonverbally shaking off what was said or done.

*Carefully consider what the return is on your investment of blowing up on people. If you do not know, be quiet and save your energy, blood pressure, heart, mind, finances, freedom, and anything else! They are not worth your precious life or resources. Vent, rage, and cry to those you trust to help you process and come back to your dignified, **UNAPOLOGETIC** roots. Please use your energies for something more constructive.*

Refer back to your notes in "A Solid Center: Your Who, What, and How" to see if any adjustments need to be made regarding your solid center to command an atmosphere of dignity for everyone.

*List ways to quickly come back to your dignified, **UNAPOLOGETIC** roots.*

_____

_____

_____

_____

_____

_____

_____

_____

_____

_____

_____

_____

_____

_____

_____

_____

_____

_____

_____

_____

_____

_____

_____

_____

_____

_____

_____

Chapter Twelve

THE ART OF UNAPOLOGETIC PROTECTION

Protect your emotions and do not wear the evidence of someone's verbal projectile vomit. Consider this: It is their personal issue that makes them so sick that they must hurl their ugly words and actions upon anyone who will pay attention. Be mindful that they are sick people. For real. However, you are not a toilet or trashcan! You are a priceless vessel who is responsible for filling yourself with good things — not someone else's illnesses. Think about this the next time someone has something insensitive to say. Their thoughts and actions are like bitter bile that they cannot contain. They heave on those who remind them of themselves or someone else. They could also be jealous of another person's freedom to be...or they could be just plain evil. Yes, the analogies may be gross, but seeing people as they are helps you to think on a more rational level.

Guard yourself and redirect them in a different direction to dump elsewhere. Depending on your response, you either did well by dodging the verbal acid bath, or you caught their infection. You know you dodged successfully when you can quickly bounce back and not be affected for a long time. You are human and have feelings, so feel what you must in order to move on. Get their poison out and off of you quickly! You know you are infected when they make you sick in your emotions, or you lose control. Remember: You can only control what goes on regarding you; not other people and not certain situations sometimes.

For many of you reading this, your first step to the art of **UNAPOLOGETIC** protection is decluttering and replacing the junk with what you know is true about you and for you. The following steps will be a little easier for you once you clear your personal space spiritually, emotionally, and mentally. Know where to draw your boundaries to defend yourself. Warning! People have tendencies to send mixed messages, so filter out the fragments that come flying towards you. Mixed messages are like a silk-covered fist—smooth in appearance, but it hits hard and wrong! They catch you off guard because you don't quite know how to take them. Respond appropriately to yourself first by deciding if that person is worth your energy. Be aware of your next line of defense. You choose whether to respond, shut them down, or walk away. Practice personal self-care to undo the sting of verbal acid splatters. This includes having a plan of things to do immediately that are positive pick-me-ups. If you are a target of attacks, I encourage you to create your own **UNAPOLOGETIC** toolkit.

Believe it or not, my pick-me-ups are what sparked my personal **UNAPOLOGETIC** toolkit. It was necessary for me to include my own personal replies and plans of action in there so that I could act accordingly the "next time." My rationale for why I am strong in the face of opposition about my stance with my gray hair toughened because of my preventative measures and my mission.

UNAPOLOGETIC Nuggets

The greatest effect of control is in your mind, heart, and spirit. Clean out the sickness of your own self-talk or any evidence of someone else's waste that has taken root within you. Your desire to protect yourself from other people's illnesses will become stronger once you have been decluttered.

*Create an **UNAPOLOGETIC** toolbox. Basic starters are: a list of pick-me-ups (special treats, activities, etc.), some inventory of pick-me-ups, and a journal to record personal replies and plans of actions to be proactive against stupidity and curiosity. Your toolbox should be healthy and constructive to build you up. It is designed to make you feel positive and confident, not vindictive, depressed, and defensive.*

*Create your **UNAPOLOGETIC** tool kit here. What do you want out of it? What pick-me-up treats and activities go in it? What other things can be added to take care of you?*

_____

_____

_____

_____

_____

_____

_____

_____

_____

_____

_____

_____

_____

_____

_____

_____

_____

_____

_____

_____

_____

_____

_____

_____

_____

_____

_____

Chapter Thirteen

UNAPOLOGETICALLY GRAY IN ACTION

My personal mission is to fly in the face of opposition to gray hair with a passion. This is not out of hatred, but to defy stinking thinking about a natural progression in life. You are probably wondering, "Why bother?" Well, for one, I have always been that *one* who people underestimated—and it broke my heart. Then, I went from being brokenhearted to becoming combative to prove my worthiness to fit in.

We often miss the target when we do not conduct ourselves in a way that is authentically us.

Now, I maintain a chilled state with a heart to simply model what I know to be true about myself and so many others. I want my lifestyle to speak louder than anything I say. I do not shrink back or hide during moments of someone's displeasure of my appearance. That is how I fly forward against critics while being myself with a quiet boldness. I just live my best life and be the picture of excellence for what people assume is something so dreadful.

I always wanted to be a model but could not make it due to my short height according to industry standards. Little did I know I was called to model something in reality that is not always regarded in a positive way to promote inspiration! This is where my identity of being chosen is so significant and has much to do with my destiny. It is my mission to make gray hair as gracefully attractive as ever!

Another reason why I do what I do is because I love people, especially those who are deemed as "undesirable" in the eyes of others. I have the ability to see things in people that most cannot because they will not get past the wrapping paper or packaging. I take sheer delight in my encounters with gifts! My compassion is much greater since I can relate to those who get overlooked and counted out. I also understand that people act like rubbish when they are treated like garbage. Once I got some healing and maturity, I realized my self-proclaimed rebellion was out of humiliation, hurt, and resentment. However, I am still thankful for it because it was a catalyst for my change. My mindset and actions have since grown into self-love, forgiveness, and confidence. What a deliverance it has been for me to replace those identity abusers with total acceptance of God's handiwork of me and my evolution! I am showcasing years' worth of work in accepting **ALL** of me and continually improving upon who I am. Being comfortable in my own skin is so beautiful and liberating! I want to see you comfortable in your own skin or you helping someone get there, too!

I must say that I am so pleased to know many sisters and brothers who are **UNAPOLOGETICALLY** embracing their gray, no matter who or what they are. I applaud you! If I can leave one of many legacies on this earth, it is to create communities in love, for love. My purpose for living **UNAPOLOGETICALLY** gray is to boost the confidence of others on the same journey, promote unity, inspire and educate, and operate with love in the presence of cynics. I, along with my silver tribe, take pride in exhibiting that gray-haired people are young at heart, strong, vibrant, healthy, attractive, and fit. Yes, contrary to what society says, the women are absolutely gorgeous with all of their sparkling glory on their heads!

For those of you on the fence about your appearance, we hope our vibes of love and life will be contagious because that is how we flow! This tribe welcomes you! We want to be accepted unconditionally for our natural appearances, just the same as you do — no matter how you look or how you came into this world.

UNAPOLOGETIC Nuggets

*Love is what makes the **UNAPOLOGETIC** world prosper. People misunderstand the purpose of gifts due to sheer ignorance or carelessness. When we do not go beyond the surface of getting to know others or do not allow people of interest to get to know us, we miss out on encountering a gift or mishandle a gift. We must see the value in people. We are richly blessed when we grasp this principle.*

*Name an **UNAPOLOGETIC** mission you can embark on that will be life-changing for you and the world. Be detailed in your response. Share it with your tribe.*

_____

_____

_____

_____

_____

_____

_____

_____

_____

_____

_____

_____

_____

_____

_____

_____

_____

_____

_____

_____

_____

_____

_____

_____

_____

_____

_____

_____

_____

Chapter Fourteen

THE UNAPOLOGETICALLY GRAY CULTURE

I want to witness a movement beyond being **UNAPOLOGETIC** as individuals and cultivate our thinking and appreciation of diversity for others. Wouldn't it be something if we all could adopt an **UNAPOLOGETICALLY** gray culture?

For example, observe the gray in hair. Gray sees no dividing lines as it gravitates to all genders, religious backgrounds, ethnicities, skin tones, ages, and economic statuses. Gray does not discriminate. If different shades of gray were people, this would explain their existence. They come from a blend of two polar opposite parents that are supposedly not considered as colors. The parenting colors are free to be themselves, yet come together to make a beautiful family created with various hues. The gray offspring follow their parents with liberated expressions of their created tones. The grays are classified as a group, just like us in the common fact that we are human beings, but not one of them is more superior than the other. Yes, some may have a stronger presence, but they can be themselves and partner with other colors on the continuum of the color palette to create harmony, no matter the environment.

That scenario is indicative of meeting in the middle with the maturity to respect and not to dislike or exclude the ones who do not share a similar likeness or pigment. We all have the same base with varying shades and energies. We could learn much from the color gray.

Similar to thinking in shades of gray instead of black and white, there is a sense of freedom in the aspect of openness to see all sides of people as they are created. If one has a different appearance, that should have no effect on anyone. Observe the "what" and "how" it is for each individual as it is in reality for *him* or *her* and move beyond the surface to discover the "who" and "why." One could make a costly mistake for not going beyond the surface to discover the deeper parts of the person of interest. How we are valued and value others make better reasoning for our thoughts about individuals and, ultimately, our choices.

UNAPOLOGETIC Nuggets

Remember that gray does not discriminate. We can all learn from the hues of gray on how to live in harmony with one another. At the end of the day, we all share the same base.

*What are your honest feelings about this chapter? Do you feel you have been inspired to accept **ALL** people, no matter their "shade of gray"?*

_____

_____

_____

_____

_____

_____

_____

_____

_____

_____

_____

_____

_____

_____

_____

_____

_____

_____

_____

_____

_____

_____

_____

_____

_____

_____

Chapter Fifteen

FORGOTTEN ETIQUETTE LESSONS

I'm going to go "there" for just a moment. Please use common sense and courtesy to stop all judgments, especially if an individual or people in your space have never done anything wrong to you. If you are going by what the media portrays or other people's experiences, you have been deceived long enough! If you have been hurt or offended, I can relate. Just know that everyone is not the same way. You know the deal. Some bad fruits occasionally appear in a great bushel. Pick them out and discard them, but do not dismiss the whole valuable bunch.

You may also have internal issues of which you are **typically** unaware. People often tend to transfer their unpleasant thoughts and behaviors onto others that stem from things they do not like about themselves.

The following exercise I am going to challenge you with ain't for weak and wimpy people. Yep, I said it! You need serious strength for this part. Are you ready?

The next time you wish to open your mouth to speak something negative about someone, practice the art of silence! There you have it!

While you are in the cancellation phase of imminent recklessness, put your mind in lockdown, too. Your thoughts are just as toxic to you internally as your spoken words and actions are externally. You poison those around you, even if they love and look up to you. Immediately ask yourself the following questions:

➢ Did the person (people) I am looking at right now ever do anything wrong to me?
➢ Where are these negative thoughts about this person (people) coming from?
➢ Are my answers valid? (Are you living through someone else's experiences or your imagination?)
➢ Does the person (people) remind me of someone, something, or an unpleasant occurrence?
➢ Does the person (people) remind me of something I do not like about myself?

I told you this exercise was not for the faint-hearted. This is your moment in the mirror. Either you choose to be in denial or use this opportunity to get a serious revelation about yourself. You can unlearn unacceptable practices. Take a chance to be and do differently. If you feel you are taking a risk outside your comfort zone, keep an open mind to look for the gift within that person. It is an acquired skill to prepare for the worst and expect the best. Suspend all negative thoughts, but also know in the back of your mind how to protect yourself in case of an unforeseen social mishap. Don't focus on any bad thoughts of what your encounter *could* be. That is faulty thinking and does not count. In essence, you have not even given the person or situation a chance. Practice mindfulness and be present in the moment. After you leave that person's presence, challenge yourself to think of at least three to five things that made your encounter a positive experience. You might be pleasantly surprised about the connections you made that you could have missed out on with your assumptions.

On the other hand, discernment is a major asset to living an **UNAPOLOGETIC** life. If you truly discern something about a person's character that is off and it is not just about their looks, you have an exception. Trust your spirit, intuition, gut, or whatever you use. You are justified. If you find you need healing from a prior offense, lean on your professional resources to get help. If you are stuck in perpetual bitterness, hatred, or stereotypical assumptions such as, "I don't know. I just don't like [fill in the blank] because [fill in the blank]..." and then start spewing verbal sewage without discernment or a valid reason... Dude! Dudette! Your unjustified aversions towards others are possibly causing you to miss out on real gifts!

This is how you can help keep a clean and harmonious environment to honor the **UNAPOLOGETIC** culture for others: Keep those toxic thoughts to yourself. Be your unapologetic self and quietly stay in your cell.

Did the last couple of statements offend you? You have just witnessed how you make others feel when you spout off whatever is in your heart and mind without thought of the impact on your listeners. Sit in your feelings, but don't put the book down yet! Take a deep breath and shake it off. You might miss something good!

Please allow me to tell you the truth with the utmost love.

Perhaps you come from places where it is acceptable to say whatever you want and however you want. It is inappropriate thinking if you have thick skin and assume everyone else should, too. I am **UNAPOLOGETICALLY** setting boundaries to show you some social etiquette and tact. You may not like what you see — and that is your prerogative — however, you can still integrate harmoniously into an **UNAPOLOGETICALLY** gray culture. Unless you have compliments that are free of any criticisms or you are attempting to prevent a social norm disaster regarding someone's appearance that may cause them public embarrassment, practice this:

DO. NOT. SAY. A. WORD.

This is your chance to put a filter on your mouth to keep from blurting out hurtful words to others who might not have a choice to look like they do. Your power and presence are so much more appreciated when you do not tear people down. In an **UNAPOLOGETICALLY** gray culture, people will always look different. Everyone understands that the uniqueness of individuals was by design, which needs no comments from you or explanations from them. No one insults the Creator or the created. Your greatest blessing could very well be tied to the person you have turned your nose up at, criticized, and dismissed.

UNAPOLOGETIC Nuggets

The best gifts are often hidden in things that seem like nothing at a glance. Do yourself a favor and do not miss out on any more treasures!

It's time to rewrite the script! Being completely honest with yourself, write negative thoughts you have about others. Then, delve deeply within to devise ways in which you will begin to apply the principles learned thus far.

_____

_____

_____

_____

_____

_____

_____

_____

_____

_____

_____

_____

_____

_____

_____

_____

_____

_____

_____

_____

_____

_____

_____

_____

_____

_____

_____

_____

Chapter Sixteen

THE ANATOMY OF AN UNAPOLOGETIC MOVEMENT

Are you feeling inspired to spark a positive **UNAPOLOGETIC** movement? Can you accept others for how they were innately fashioned? This is all about creating communities in love, for love. It is time out for ganging up to cause hurt, division, and hatred against others. It is unfortunate that we must step up to set examples because people in authority are abusing their power by publicly attacking people's appearances. We have too many wounded people who are withdrawn or have conformed to living unauthentic lives to fit in among people who may not accept them anyway. We all were created with love to share love in our own individual ways.

Can't find your tribe? Start one! You have something special to give that others are waiting for. It might be on a very small scale, or it could be worldwide! There are people who are waiting for you to do this.

[96]

How would you create **UNAPOLOGETIC** communities in love, for love? What are you **UNAPOLOGETIC** about and why? Who else has this in common with you? What will the make-up of your group be like? Where else will you find your people? What does your group stand for? Is it private or community-oriented? Is it a social gathering? An advocacy? A support group? Will there be particular goals or specific plans for the group (i.e., travel, education, community service, etc.)?

What is your personality like to facilitate a community? For introverts who do not do well with groups, you can be a voice all by yourself that draws others to your platform via podcasts or radio. You are in a better space to empower and encourage others who are where you have been. You might even write a book about your experiences or desires. You have a voice that may touch a different audience that others cannot reach. Many people do successful blogs, vlogs, and events.

For extroverts who do not mind gatherings, you can start groups in your community, workplace, religious organizations, and other establishments, or even online all over the world. The most popular venues are networking groups that also function as support groups, which are done both virtually and in person. The whole hashtag (#) utilization in social media and your writings will be huge for getting your **UNAPOLOGETIC** movement noticed. Be creative with your hashtags and add them to your digital correspondence. Someone will type it in and see everything your group is up to.

The purpose of an **UNAPOLOGETIC** movement is to advance onward in total wellness, awareness, and self-confidence, but with a different twist. We have a dire need for more communities to be created that exhibit love on the inside and outside. When gathering a group together (no matter the size), I would recommend setting some agreements which everyone collectively creates and approves. So many people often skip this critical step—one that could prevent so much drama and misunderstandings. You might think you shouldn't have to go *there*, but there are always people who feel they must haul their garbage wherever they go. Basic agreements usually center around the following:

> ➢ The basis of the group, what it stands for, and activities to participate in.
> ➢ Zero tolerance for dissension, cliques, and conflicts during meeting times.
> ➢ A common regard for people, regardless of similarities or differences.
> ➢ Respect for one's self, one another internally, and others externally.
> ➢ Cohesiveness and inclusiveness.
> ➢ Ways to stretch and challenge one another to do and be their best selves.
> ➢ Nurturing those who want to grow into their own authenticity path.

Be aware that your **UNAPOLOGETIC** movement will attract some severely broken people! Many people who have been disregarded and damaged often have different intentions when it comes to being **UNAPOLOGETIC** in the right perspective. Some broken people come to mend and get help, while others hurt people. Immature and wounded people see it as a license to be uninhibited without respect to themselves or others. Spend quality time and really get to know people and their motives. See how the group can be of benefit. Any or all members have the right to assess if the person is willing to grow or stay stuck in pain. All members are clear that they are not counselors or dumping grounds for someone who harbors internal illnesses for whatever reasons. Everyone stands united with empathetic firmness as they assist the person within the scope of the organization's agreements. The group unanimously decides with the person whether to help him or her move forward to be healthy or how to be supportive as the person seeks professional help or other forms of care. Consistency in abiding by member principles, along with clarity of the movement's goodwill threshold, can nudge the hurting person to make an important decision. The person has a choice to leave offended, remain in the group, or return at a better time. This is an example of a group setting firm and loving boundaries without making the person feel excluded. Scenarios like these call for some ground rules, so that impartiality and confusion do not disrupt a good vibe or spoil the purpose of the movement.

Notice how the whole group owns this **UNAPOLOGETIC** movement. There should be no dictatorship of any kind, not even from the one who initiates the group. The initiator does have the right to oversee the flow of the movement and maintain the leadership base if it grows exponentially. A movement is not from or about one person only. It requires several people to get on board and roll ahead. Everyone alternates being facilitators and contributors to keep the energy alive. The group should be on one accord to boot out anyone who causes division, conflict, or destructive activities that threaten to change the dynamic of the group. Exercise your **UNAPOLOGETIC** right to protect the organization at all costs. This is about a positive movement. There is nothing worse than one or a few out of control people who mess up a good cause. We all know the deal. It takes just one negative person to poison and dismantle the whole group. Each person should have something constructive to bring to the group that will benefit everyone involved. Established mutual goals may include that members are well-connected, interactive, uphold a safe space with fun, build each other up, be a united front to critics with grace and maturity, and show impartiality to others in their presence. It can be a private group that always meets behind closed doors. However, there is nothing greater than having an outing where everyone represents in full force with class. It is an attention-getter that sparks curiosity, especially when the group is confident and living life **UNAPOLOGETICALLY**. Those who are friendly are invited in to hang out with a cool group of people whom they may find very invigorating. In case there is a social mishap, the group bands together to decide how to command an atmosphere of dignity while protecting one another.

Remember: No one has to get on the level of ignorance with those who want to act out. You do not take abuse, but you also represent communities in love, for love.

It is time to reverse the negative images of people and features that are erroneously portrayed by the media, along with the accompaniment of snobbery and unjust preferential treatment against those who do not deserve it. Individuals or small gangs that tarnish an entire group with their antics also need to stop. When people are disgusted inside or outside of your group, you are rallying offensively in an unapologetic way. Revamp your group or shut it down to avoid serious issues.

The rumblings of your **UNAPOLOGETIC** movement have the potential to become so powerful that it gains the attention of those who observe or hear about it. People might want to become a part of the movement, even though they have nothing in common. The reality of people wanting to join who do not fit the group profile is a probable sign that you may be doing something right. I say that lightly, depending on the cause or people's motives.

Give the media something to pick up and get your shine on! An altruistic **UNAPOLOGETIC** movement extends out into the community with something positive to give to others. The blessing in this is that those who are not a part of your group can promote the goodness of your **UNAPOLOGETIC** movement. This is an opportunity to silence the critics while revealing what they are too blind to see. As people are in your company, they witness personally who you really are, not just your appearance or what you do.

So, what happens if you don't like the discrimination regarding something you are **UNAPOLOGETIC** for? There is strength in numbers. The best place to hit people is in their wallets and reputation, but it must be done strategically and with exactitude:

➤ Do things in a peaceful manner that commands attention.

> ➢ If you spread the word about an incident, please be truthful and stick to the facts.
> ➢ Boycott, start petitions, and show up at meetings in droves, but do it with class. You want your message to be heard in the right way. Protests done in combative ways with ignorance is far from the **UNAPOLOGETIC** way. Being able to boldly be yourself, protect yourself and your rights, and not be obnoxious about it is the correct way.
> ➢ There is a time and place for aggressiveness, but it is only as an extreme last resort.
> ➢ Make sure you do not risk any legal repercussions — unless you are prepared to go through with the consequences.

I am hopeful that something is truly stirring within you to either be one or all of the following:

> ➢ Be strong with your **UNAPOLOGETIC** life in a positive way;
> ➢ Be the voice for an **UNAPOLOGETIC** group; or
> ➢ Unite with others as an **UNAPOLOGETIC** force to be reckoned with.

I believe with all my heart that each one can reach one until individuals, families, communities, and ultimately, the nation can be changed to stop this petty foolishness about people's appearances. The initial step is to be confident in who you are, why you are, and how you are. Find your tribe in order to be equipped to stand assured in your unique existence.

Can you be authentically you without being offensive? Then advance beyond yourself and practice being an inspiration to others.

Will you be that one who creates a safe place to nurture those who have been wounded and not contaminate them with more bitterness?

To those of you who have been strengthened, are you strong enough to reach out to others and help them be confident?

Are you able to stand in the face of ignorance with all manners of intelligence, protect yourself as necessary, and maintain an atmosphere of dignity for all?

If you answered "YES!" to all of those questions, you have the potential to be the leader needed to get an **UNAPOLOGETIC** party started!

In Conclusion...

Hello again My Love,

Our time together was not coincidental. This is your time to rise above your negative thoughts from the destructive actions of others who affected you. I hope you found your safe place to rewrite the script of your life.

Living **UNAPOLOGETICALLY** will take some getting used to but trust me; it will get easier. Any investment of you living an **UNAPOLOGETIC** life is my answered prayer for you. What you do with your harvest of living your best life authentically is all up to you. I challenge you to do it confidently in a society that is so quick to reject people based on appearances. You deserve it, and so does the rest of the world!

There is not exactly a cookie-cutter resolution for this process because you know what is best for you and your life. The passageways to self-awareness and healing regarding your life will be completely different than mine. You are a trailblazer in your own right. You have something wonderful to show us. The world will be blessed by the **UNAPOLOGETIC** culture you demonstrate.

I model being **UNAPOLOGETIC** on a daily basis and consider it a privilege. I cannot wait until our paths cross! You are *that* gift I am waiting to encounter!

Love,

About the Author

Traci Byerly considers herself as a late-bloomer in life, but it is better late than never! She spent a major part of her adult life exercising her wings in learning patience, tenacity, and resilience. Through much prayer, inner nourishment, and critical mindset changes, she rose above unresolved traumatic experiences, poor self-esteem, misfortunes beyond her control, and the consequences of unwise choices.

In her late 40's, Traci began to achieve dreams she once thought were only fantasies. She received her Master's Degree in Social Work with an emphasis in Mental Health and obtained licensing as a Master Social Worker. She is a Model, Author, and Certified Life Coach. Traci holds an International Coach Federation (ICF) credential as an Associate Certified Coach (ACC). She is slowly pursuing her clinical license to become a therapist in the future. Traci married the man of her dreams, Fredrick, and they are *STILL* on their honeymoon! When they are not working hard and doing ministry, they love to travel and enjoy life together. Her dreams are still coming true! She is an inspiration of faith for those who have lost hope in their visions. Her message is never to give up, no matter your age, circumstances, or other barriers!

Traci's heart's desire was to always be a model, but she was too short. She now understands her modeling dreams had a larger, divine purpose: She is called to be an influential picture of healthier lifestyle choices in every "...ally" of life (e.g., spiritually, mentally, physically, relationally, financially, etc.). Her dedication is towards the empowerment and advancement of women and girls.

A glimpse of her passionate missions includes: teaching self-love beyond external appearances; demonstrating value of the whole person and not just body parts, personas, performances, and possessions; exemplifying social and intelligent conduct; growth in prosperity and wellness; and restoration of all appropriate protection, rights, and dignity. Traci is serious about her life's purpose to make a difference wherever she goes. Her heart's desire is for people to leave her presence in a better state than when they first encountered her.

Traci and Fredrick share one son, three daughters, and a grandson. They reside in the Dallas/Fort Worth, Texas area.

Connect with
Traci Byerly

For more information on Traci Byerly regarding:

Speaking engagements or other bookings:
Website: www.tracibyerly.com
Email: tracibyerly@gmail.com

Coaching Services:
Website: www.yourchosenpass.com

Mailing Correspondence:
Traci Byerly
P.O. Box 161716
Fort Worth, TX 76161

Social Media:
Facebook.com/traci.demossbyerly
Facebook.com/YourChosenPass
Instagram.com - @tracibyerly

Made in the USA
Las Vegas, NV
31 May 2022

49618755R00070